Positiv

MW01290575

Overcome Negativity &

Become A Happier, More

Positive Person

Jane Aniston

Table of Contents

- Tolerance

- Resilience

- Persistence

- Charity

- Love

Chapter 2-Getting Rid Of the Negatives

What Is Negative Thinking?

Character Traits of Negative Thinkers

How Negative Thinking Paralyzes

How to Deal With Negative Habits

Chapter 3- Training Your Brain to Think Positively

Pray

Meditate

Play

Write

Speak

Read

Visualize

Practice Compassion

Laugh

Smile

Chapter 4- When Positive Can Be Negative

Misconceptions About Positive Thinking

Situation where positive thinking will not work

Achieving a Balance

Chapter 5- Exercises In Positive Thinking

With Family

At Work

When Facing Tough Times

Setting a Daily of Thinking Positively

<u>Introduction</u>

Have you ever wondered why some people just seem to have it all? Or, how some people may *not* have it all, but act like they do? In other words, why are some people just plain happy? In spite of the challenges and setbacks we all go through, they just always seem to be upbeat and "high on life".

These people, who always have an inner joy and remain calm and in control are *positive thinkers*. They're not perfect but they enjoy life and their happiness and enthusiasm can easily rub off on us. They leave us happy and smiling. They're great both with people and at what they do.

These people have discovered the secret to what it's like to always see the glass half-full and to be able to find that pot of gold at the end of the rainbow. They charge through life and weather the blows; always emerging seemingly unscathed and still with feet planted firmly on the ground.

Studies have proven that positive thinking can have a long-term and advantageous effect on our lives. Some people may be naturally inclined to being positive, while others may not. But positive thinking is a mental muscle that can be flexed, exercised and trained. You can tap into your inner positivity in order to both feel better and to give yourself the best chance of achieving success.

As you leaf through the pages of this book, you'll find out what it means to think positively, what it is that may be hindering you from being happy, and how to react positively in different situations. When you learn to maintain positive thoughts, you're likely to see some truly amazing benefits, such as improved health, increased competence, a reduction in stress-levels, feeling happier and even looking younger!

Chapter 1

Looking on the Bright Side

What is positive thinking?

Positive thinking is, simply put, an attitude of looking at things from a positive perspective; seeing the proverbial glass as half-full rather than half-empty; looking on the bright side of life. But this does not imply that one should try to escape from reality and deny the truth. It may be referred to as a discipline that allows the mind to anticipate the good that could come out of any situation. It is not a blind fantasizing, it a choice of thoughts that can be beneficial to the thinker. One thing is for certain, it's definitely a way of thinking that can improve one's life. Through positive thinking, one can look beyond the current circumstances and anticipate a resolution in the future. A positive thinker is able to find strength and hope in even the most difficult of circumstances.

Some may have the impression that positive thinking is simply "being happy" or cheerful. There is actually more to it than that. A truly positive outlook requires mindfulness and restraint. It involves the ability to think and act constructively even when one's emotions may dictate otherwise. It involves recognizing negative and destructive thought patterns or habits and using learned techniques to change them into positive ones. Sometimes optimism and positive thinking are interchanged, but optimism is more of an emotion while positive thinking is a belief. So, positive thinking is never a forced emotion.

Positive thinking has become very popular because of its relevance to the modern way of life. The fast-paced and pressure-packed lifestyle of today requires clever counter—maneuvering on our part. Positive thinking has become the key to maintaining happiness and success in our careers, our relationships and our overall well-being.

The Benefits of Positive Thinking

.

Studies prove that positive thinkers are not only happier, but also healthier. I remember a "faith healer" who claimed to be able to remove kidney, gallbladder stones, tumors and what not from people who sought healing. He was a quack and his conscience had caught up with him. He eventually admitted to lying and to using organs from pigs to appear to come out from his patients' bodies. When he was asked why some of his patients claimed to have been healed, he responded that they had been healed by their own belief – by the power of their minds. This shows how powerful a tool the mind can be if we can harness it. The mind no doubt influences the body. Positive thinking influences the mind, resulting in better health, better immunity and a longer lifespan.

There are many ways by which positive thinking affects our bodies and minds in good ways. Here are just some:

A longer lifespan

A Dutch study found pessimistic people more likely to die by 55% during the time they were being studied. Positive thinkers live longer, more fulfilling lives.

Slower aging

A Canadian study on people 60 years and older found positive thinkers did not show mobility and functional problems as early as the negative-thinkers. The pessimists were 80% more likely to develop problems, compared to the optimists.

Lower cholesterol

In 2013, a study done by the Harvard School of Public Health showed their middle-age participants who tested as optimistic in tests also had high levels of "good cholesterol" in their blood.

Stronger immunity

Being negative has been shown in studies to make one more susceptible to the cold and flu. Positive thinkers have stronger immune responses as a general rule.

Reduced risk of cardiovascular disease

A study published in a journal of the American Heart Association found that positive thinkers were less likely to develop coronary heart disease. Another study cited that optimists had 73% less chances of heart failure. It was mentioned, though, that optimistic people tend to take care of themselves and follow a healthy lifestyle, which could explain these figures. Whether directly or indirectly, positivity still has a strong correlation to reduced risk.

Better coping skills

Remaining positive during periods of stress helped adults and teenagers alike to cope. Teenagers were found to be better at avoiding depression, substance abuse and antisocial behavior.

Higher income

The positive thinker takes active steps to improve his life and is generally more persistent in his studies or in getting an education and therefore is more likely to get a high income.

Better view of options and possibilities

The positive thinker was found to be able to come up with more options and possibilities in their plans. The emotions brought about by positive thinking encourage openness to how experiences can be benefited from in the future.

Increased skills and talents

Again, positive emotions associated with positive thinking can motivate one to pursue and develop new skills and talents. These skills can be useful later in life, not just temporarily.

Enhanced attractiveness

Positive thinking generates an energy in us that makes us more likely to smile, have a better posture, a more confident gait and a sparkle in our eyes. Positivity radiates and catches people's attention. Positive thinkers also tend to take care of their grooming and the way they present themselves to others.

Improved performance in sports

An athlete needs to have self-confidence and must practice positive thinking to attain his goal and to persevere with the effort required for developing skills. Many athletes rely on positive thinking to do well. They must believe in their own abilities and in their ability to win.

More friends

Positive thinkers exude confidence. Positive emotions are contagious, so people feel happy around positive thinkers. People enjoy being with positive thinkers and they feel energized by them. Other people can easily spot and are attracted to genuinely happy and positive people.

Better careers

Attitude can have a huge impact on one's career. Thinking positively will prepare you to respond appropriately during trying times. You will be more prepared to take on and complete tasks and accomplish goals.

Stronger marriages

Many conflicts between spouses stem from negative thoughts. Remember, positive thinking involves the control or removal of negative thought patterns and habits. By practicing positive thinking, one will learn to be a kind, understanding and loving spouse. Trust and communication will be developed.

As you can see, developing the habit of positive thinking will generate a beneficial energy that will permeate through to all facets of life. You may be interested in developing the habit of positive thinking for one particular purpose; to improve performance in a sport, for example. However, the fact is that this will also send ripples of positive energy to almost all areas of your life.

Traits of Positive Thinkers

What did the likes of Gandhi, Helen Keller, Maya Angelou, Mother Theresa, Thomas Edison and Nelson Mandela have in common? They were all positive thinkers. These are people who overcame unimaginable odds and inspired the world. It was no doubt their positivity that helped them through all the difficulties they had to endure. In spite of all the negatives that life threw at them, they remained steadfast and emerged as shining examples of what can be done when one has the right mindset.

What was it about them that made them shine? The greats of the past and of the present day all share common traits. By the way, great may not mean rich, it simply means that they succeeded in instilling hope in others, in using whatever means they had to influence those around them and around the world positively and bringing about changes for the greater good. Here are some of the traits of positive thinkers:

Focus

Positive thinkers keep their focus. They have definite, clearly-set goals. They look beyond the circumstances they are currently experiencing and move towards their goal.

Vision

This goes hand-in-hand with focus. Positive thinkers see possibilities and the bigger picture. They are creative, imaginative and innovative. They are exciting to talk to because you feel their passion and determination in achieving their vision.

Optimism

If you look into the lives of many high-achievers, you'll often find that they have been through the harshest possible experiences at some point during their life. Some were in concentration camps, some were raped, abandoned, discriminated upon or tortured. Incredibly enough, they still saw the bright side. Positive thinkers choose to be victors instead of victims.

Integrity

Their strength of character is always evident. They tend do things with honesty and with conviction. They do not sacrifice ethics and values just to achieve success.

Belief or Faith

They do not lose faith in humanity and many have a strong belief in some kind of higher power. They believe even when their dreams have not yet been reached.

Persistence

Positive thinkers just don't give up. They don't let setbacks or failures pull them down. They continue on because they know they can achieve their goal. They see obstacles as opportunities to learn and to grow.

Resilience

This quality stems from persistence. When trials come, our positive thoughts may wane. But positive thinkers face difficulties with courage, get back on their feet and continue moving forward. Positive thinkers focus on finding solutions and even helping others in a crisis.

Courage

Positive thinkers weigh the cost and are aware of the risks involved in their decisions or activities. But they are willing take risks and to face their fears.

Balance

They know and value balance in their lives. Even though they are excited to fulfill their dreams, they know that they must maintain a healthy balance and find time for relationships and for keeping their inner peace.

Charity

They are open-minded, respectful and tolerant of others' beliefs. They share their ideas, know-how and skills. Positive thinkers are not lacking in sympathy as they may have experienced suffering themselves. Many put up foundations or give to those who are in need or who are going through the same hardships that they went through.

Love

Positive people are driven by love. They are willing to work hard for the good of others. They are willing to leave their comfort zones in order to help others. They give of themselves unselfishly and passionately in whatever they do. The thing that drives them to strive more is the knowledge that what they do will benefit others.

We have gone over the benefits of positive thinking and the traits of those who practice it. As you can see, positive thinking will make you healthier, more attractive, happier and better able to maximize your potential. The qualities mentioned may not come naturally to you, but they can be learned and developed. Through positive thinking, you can learn to embody these traits. It isn't impossible.

Chapter 2

Getting Rid Of the Negatives

What Is Negative Thinking?

When you dwell on how things can go wrong or you fail to see good in anything, that is negative thinking. You have to recognize negative thought patterns and habits in order to change them. Sometimes we think negatively without being aware of it. Negative thinking can be better understood by getting familiar with the common negative thought processes.

Filtering or disqualifying the positives

This is when one filters out all the good things and focuses or lays emphasis only on the bad. It's seeing only that speck on the otherwise pristine sheet of paper. The birthday party was a success, the food was great, the children were happy, the magician was amazing, and the celebrant was exuberant. But all you can think about is the balloons – you ordered 5 colors, but you were only given 3. This ruined the whole party for you.

Polarizing or "all-or-nothing" thinking

Everything is black or white, good or bad. You make one mistake and you write yourself off as a failure.

Catastrophizing

Always believing that the WORST will happen. You see some hair falling off your head and you immediately assume you'll be bald the next day.

Personalizing

Believing that you are the cause of the bad things that happen; that people are blaming everything on you. The office outing was canceled because you'd be there and nobody wanted to go with you around.

Self-Labeling

"I'm stupid."

"I'm ugly."

"I'm not a likable person."

This is when you're the first to put yourself down.

Mind-Reading

Mind readers really believe that they can tell what people are thinking. This dialogue illustrates this pattern:

Wife: Everyone hates me at work.

Husband: What? Nonsense! You're a wonderful person. Just give them time to get to know you better. Why do you think that anyway; what did they say to you?

Wife: Nothing, they didn't say anything. I just know it. I'm sure of it!

Some of the examples here may sound amusing, but negative though patterns will block your chances of achieving success and happiness in life. Pay attention to where you might be falling into these traps.

Habits of Negative Thinkers

Don't be surprised if some of the traits here are ones that you've always thought were good.

Striving for nothing less than perfect

You've always been taught to do your best. But negative thinkers can't stop at their best, they seek perfection. As you know, perfection is not always achievable, so seeking perfection in everything will only set you up for disappointment and frustration.

Time travel

You're always thinking of things that happened in the past or things you wish for in the future, you forget the here and now. The past can no longer be changed and the future would be brighter if you focused on making things right in the now. Sometimes you put off time for yourself, intending to do it in the future. Unfortunately, it gets put off for far too long. Although looking towards the future can give you direction, too much "dreaming" without actual action will not yield any results.

Keeping up with the Joneses

You thought a little "friendly" competition was healthy so you make sure you're keeping up with your neighbor, your classmate, your co-worker, a sibling or even your spouse. Another sure-fire way to frustration. There will always be someone better than you and you'll be missing out on what really is best for you.

Focusing on what could go wrong

It seems right to consider all the possible negative consequences of your decisions or actions. But over-dwelling on the possible negative outcomes could fill you with fear and prevent you from exploring and taking risks.

Garbage in, garbage out

Watching depressing news reports and TV dramas that are filled with anger and sadness; reading stories or articles that feed more negative emotions; being with people who are always quick to blame and criticize; and staying in a stressful, noisy, polluted environment. All the negatives that you take in will affect you and, most likely, you'll be sending out negative vibes as well.

All eyes on you

Not. The truth is people are too busy with their own issues and problems to pay too much attention. Don't worry about what other people might say (even though your mom told you to). Negative thinkers try to restrict actions or they refrain from expressing their thoughts for fear of what others might say or think.

Pessimism

This is when you dwell on what can't instead of what can; when you see the bad in every situation and you believe the worst will happen.

"I can't. "

 "It's not possible."

" We'll never make it."

"I don't want to be too happy right now because I'm sure something bad will happen after this."

How Negative Thinking Paralyzes

It is interesting to understand how negative thoughts and habits affect us. The effect of negative thinking goes all the way back to when man had to hunt and their environment was full of dangerous wild beasts.

As a survival mechanism, when we are confronted with fear, we somehow lose perspective and our focus becomes limited. In the past, facing up to danger caused our brains to signal us to DROP EVERYTHING and to either fight or take flight. Everything else was set aside. There was no time to think, analyze or explore options. The brain said: DANGER! GET READY FOR A FIGHT, OR FLEE!

We no longer face as many dangers or wild beasts as men did in the past. However, our brains have still retained this primitive survival mechanism. Therefore, we become paralyzed when confronted by fear and when negative thoughts take a hold of us. Our brains shut everything out and turn off the sectors that control our explorative and innovative abilities. In other words, when we think negatively, our vision is narrowed and we lose sight of our options.

How to Deal With Negative Habits

Now that we know how negative thinking works in the brain, we must learn how to counteract negative thought patterns and habits. As you go further in this book, you will become acquainted with practical steps to combat negative thinking. For now let's take a look at some general pointers on handling it.

You can do it!

You're your own best friend. As your own best friend, you should be the first to believe in yourself. Know that you can make a positive contribution in this world.

Make a list of your assets

You may feel useless or talentless. Draw up a list of good things about yourself. Maybe you're a good listener, a good dancer, or a friendly person. You'll be surprised at how much you actually can do and how you underestimate yourself. If you can't do it, ask some close friends to tell you what your good points are. Whenever you're confronted by a negative thought, counteract with one of your assets.

Have some clear-cut goals

They may be simple goals, but the key here is that you'll know when to stop and when you've achieved them. It will give you a sense of achievement. Also, by setting deadlines, you resist the urge to do things too "perfectly." Learning to meet deadlines and instead focus on the basic requirements can help uncomplicate your life. Striving for excellence isn't wrong; it's the pursuit of the unattainable however that only results in frustration.

Do some positive self-talk

Talk to yourself positively. This helps prep your mind and counteract the negative voices in and around you. "I can do this!"

Immerse yourself in the positive

Surround yourself with positives – positive people, a healthy environment, relaxing music, inspirational books, heartwarming movies, etc. Fill your surroundings with people and things that will fill you with positive emotions. Remember, when you are filled with positive emotions, possibilities open up.

Take responsibility for your life

Stand by your decisions. If you make mistakes, acknowledge your mistakes, learn from them and move on. Instead of dwelling on your problems, make a plan and take action to solve them. Your past and the mistakes or people who influenced you in the past no longer have a hold on you. Your life is in your hands.

Act the part

You may not feel confident and self-assured, but you can fake it. Act the part and you can fool your brain into believing that you ARE confident. It may make you feel deceitful at first, but in time you'll find that you aren't acting anymore.

I'm sure that by now you've probably identified some of your own negative habits. Follow the tips to become a more confident and positive person and you'll begin to see changes in your life. Take out a notebook and work through the ideas in this chapter. Write down where you are selling yourself short or tripping yourself up and how you plan to rectify this. Check in regularly to assess your progress.

This is just the start. As previously mentioned, positive thinking is a muscle that needs a lot of exercise to be developed. Read on.

Chapter 3

Training Your Brain to Think Positively

There are concrete steps to developing positive thinking. If you need to follow a specific regimen at the gym to develop specific muscle groups, it's the same with developing positive thinking. It may seem forced at first but, later and with much practice, your brain will produce positive thoughts effortlessly and gracefully. Here are some practical steps you can take to build this positivity muscle!

Meditate (...or pray)

Research has proven that people who meditate daily are more positive. Positive emotions always nurture long-term skills. Three months through the study, people who meditated were observed to be more emotionally stable and less sickly. Meditation makes your body release "good" hormones and strengthens you physically.

Find a method that works for you. For some, simply having a few moments of silence once a day is enough. Others use it as a time to ponder on inspirational or religious ideas. Others listen to relaxing music and simply use the time to ease their mind. You could close your eyes and practice deep breathing exercises. It doesn't have to be elaborate. A complicated meditation routine might be too discouraging or difficult to maintain. It could simply mean sitting quietly at the breakfast table with a cup of tea.

You may not believe in prayer, but many have found it an excellent way to sort out one's thoughts – to focus on the positive and push out the negatives. Meditation is when your body and mind are at one in focusing on positive truths and emotions like joy, peace, love, courage and gratitude.

Play

It is during play that children develop skills for life. The positive emotions that accompany play are rich media for growth. The benefits are not limited to children. Adults should also set aside time to engage in enjoyable activities and feed on the positive emotions that they generate.

Sometimes adults feel they must put off fun activities and focus on their career or education to build skills and to achieve success. The good news is that the skills are developed during play. Happiness and other positive emotions are what will push you to succeed. And success also brings more positive feelings. So don't be afraid to take time to have fun and feel happy.

Play doesn't actually have to happen as something separate from work or your other "grown-up activities". Play can be incorporated in work and in relationships. Play doesn't have to be just an activity.

It should be an attitude – to feel excitement and anticipation in what you do and to remove the barriers of having to impress or compete for a prize.

Write

A study published by the Journal of Research in Personality found that writing about a positive experience for three months was enough to improve the participants' emotional and physical states.

Purposely taking a few minutes every day to write about an inspiring thought, observation or experience can help reinforce your brain's focus on the positive. Again, start out with just a few sentences each day. This activity doesn't have to be a grueling writing exercise. It's just a time set aside to put down in writing any positive experiences you've had during the day. Writing itself is helpful and, additionally, you can go back to your entries later and remind yourself of those positive experiences. It will help you during those times when you may not feel so positive.

Speak

The power of the spoken word cannot be overlooked. There's a lot of negativity around us. We hear negative words and ideas through the media, through articles or news reports, and from the people around us. Worst of all, we hear it from ourselves. Some of us may have developed the habit of putting ourselves down. Without thinking, we automatically call ourselves "stupid" or "hopeless." We forget that this all adds on top of the other negativity we're receiving.

Experts say it helps to choose words that carry more positivity. Instead of just saying "fine," say "great" or "wonderful." Talk to yourself as if you were your own best friend. Give yourself some pep talk. Don't say anything to yourself that you would say to other people.

Listen to yourself and watch for any negative words or phrases you may unconsciously be using too frequently. A few negatives is not a really anything to be worried about, it's the ones you say over and over again that penetrate your consciousness and may eventually become reality.

As strange as it may sound, it's been proven that our consciousness hears the words we say and does not recognize negation. When you say "I'm not sick," all that registers is "sick." Say "I'm not feeling well" and your consciousness hears "well." This creates a positive picture in your mind.

Here are some examples of negative phrases changed into positive ones:

Negative: I failed.

Positive: I wasn't successful.

Negative: It's too drastic.

Positive: Let's try it!

Negative: I'm tired.

Positive: I need some rest.

Negative: I'm so bored!

Positive: I need to do something

exciting.

Read

Find books and articles on positive thinking. Fill your mind with ideas, facts and advice about it. This is essential to filling your mind with positives. Having a book that you can refer to once in a while can serve to refresh you during times when you are feeling down. There may be too much information on the Internet, with much of it being contradictory and confusing. Stop when the effect on you is becoming negative, and go back to the basics. Later, when you've gained more mastery in composing your thoughts and emotions, you may continue searching for inspiring testimonies, readings and advice. You will have to discern what to believe and what not to.

Visualize

Successful people know the power of visualization. They know that using mental images has tremendous influence on achieving goals. When we worry, we are producing mental images of things that can go wrong. We can counter this by visualizing our desired outcome. Call it day dreaming, but it can be a sensible part of the process of planning or of creating a strategy. Visualizing helps you rehearse what could happen in your mind and prepare you for possible challenges. Medical practitioners recognize the value of visualizing to overcome phobias, reduce pain, improve performance in sports or achieve healing form disease. Athletes are especially familiar with visualization and its effectiveness.

There are three requisites in visualization: you must be completely relaxed, you must engage all the senses (hear, feel, see, smell and taste in your mind) while visualizing and you must practice over and over again.

Practice Compassion

Find time to purposefully do something good for others. It doesn't have to be anything too grand. You must train yourself to be sensitive to the needs of others and to do what you can to help. This requires a conscious effort to remove focus from the self and to direct it towards others. Ancient Tibetans believed that exercising compassion gives you power to release little miracles into the world. Compassion offers benefits to both the giver and the receiver. It fills both with joy, love and warmth. These are very positive emotions that condition you into being a better, more skillful and successful person.

Laugh

Laughter truly is the best medicine. Humor helps melt away the negativity from your system and helps you to move into pure, unadulterated joy. Laughter and humor are now used for patients suffering from severe illnesses. It has been proven to alleviate suffering in cancer patients. It is said to improve blood circulation and strengthen the heart. When you laugh, your body releases endorphins that relieve pain and give you a sense of well-being. It also strengthens the immune system.

Laughter works so well in breaking down stress and dissolving tension, and definitely produces positive emotions.

Smile

Smiling is another way to relieve stress. Smiling to yourself in the mirror sends a signal to your brain that things are just fine. We can actually "fool" our brains into thinking things are okay by smiling. Smiling actually sets off a rewiring in the brain that results in the release of positive emotions. You can even fake a smile and still get the same positive results. Others look positively on people who are smiling and see them as courteous and competent individuals. Smiling not only releases positive thoughts in you but also in others around you.

It is possible to overcome your negative thought patterns but it will require conscious effort on your part on many levels. As you see, becoming a positive thinker requires us to exercise all of our senses and to saturate ourselves with positive stimuli.

How could you incorporate the ideas into your life on a regular basis? Take out a notebook and make a plan of the actions you're going to take in order to increase the number of positive thoughts and feelings you experience.

Chapter 4

When Positive Can Be Negative

Misconceptions about positive thinking

Some may scoff at the belief in positive thinking and see it as a kind of hocus-pocus pseudoscience. It is important to clarify this matter. There are things that should be made clear about positive thinking:

- It does not involve some magic spells, rituals or powers.

- It is not about having unrealistic goals or expectations.

- It involves looking at things positively yet realistically.

- Positive thinking goes hand-in-hand with positive action.

That being said, there are times when all the positive thinking in the world will not work. Do I sound negative right now? These are truths that will help us avoid having unreasonable expectations that will only frustrate us in the end. In order to move onto success, it is a positive action to identity and face the obstacles.

Obstacles to positive thinking

Denying your fears and not facing reality

Positive thinkers have the courage to face their fears because they know that it must be done in order for a positive change to happen. A person who denies that he feels pain in his abdomen because he wants to be "positive" about it may just as well end up in the ER for appendicitis or worse. Positive thinking means looking our challenge square in the face and knowing you will be able to overcome them. The positive thinker would have had a checkup and would know that he could take medication and measures to make everything all right.

Thinking positive thoughts but not doing anything about it

Positive thinking is not mindless dreaming and wishing, then sitting around waiting for it to be dropped in your lap. Positive thinking is knowing that you can dream and then take steps to achieve that dream. The dream is possible only with positive action.

Believing that positive thinking means nothing bad will ever happen to you

Positive thinking means facing up to your fears and finding solutions. It means facing the reality that bad things can happen but that you will still be fine in the end. It's knowing that sometimes bad feelings can be triggers for us to become better and for us to develop solutions to our problems. It means we can have hope in spite of the losses, hurdles or difficulties we encounter in life.

Not knowing what you want

If you believe you can just smile and laugh, but you don't have any visions or dreams, this is not positive thinking. Positive thinkers have a clear vision and are always moving toward their goals by taking positive steps to achieve them.

Expecting things to happen exactly the way you want

Expecting things to happen only the way you want may lead to you missing the positive outcome you desire. You may have dreamed of a mansion but you only got an apartment and feel that you wasted your time thinking positively. Positive thinkers are flexible and recognize good things when they come. When things do not turn out as expected, positive thinkers do not wallow in disappointment. They are flexible and grateful for all the great things that come their way.

Unknowingly focusing on the negative

One may simply say that they are positive but not truly deal with the negatives in their life. There may be negative emotions still dominating your thoughts and impeding the actions you will allow yourself to take in order to achieve your goals. You may say "I forgive my no-good, philandering cheater of a husband and I'm thinking positively now." Sounds like the bitterness and hurt has not been dealt with yet. This is an obstacle to achieving success.

Achieving a Balance

Positive thinking should in no way diminish our drive to achieve our dreams. It should drive us and push us toward out goals. The obstacles to the effectiveness of positive thinking tend to slow us down. Misguided understanding of positive thinking leads some to lose their momentum towards success. Some believe that positive thinking means sitting back to let the universe deliver whatever it is that they desire.

To achieve a balance, we must not lose sight of the other side of positive thinking – and that is positive action. Because positive thinking promotes happy and pleasurable emotions, we tend to think that it is all about enjoyment and relaxation. It may seem unpleasant, but becoming a success while employing positive thinking still requires that we face up to the obstacles that are currently in our way and devise concrete steps to overcome them. However, the positive thinker will have at his disposal the benefits of a clearer, sharper, more motivated and creative mind as well as a healthier, more energetic body.

Chapter 5

Exercises In Positive Thinking

Exercise, exercise, exercise! The benefits of exercise cannot be discounted. It is the same with positive thinking. You must exercise forming positive thoughts and pushing out the negative until it becomes second nature. As we have learned in Chapter 1, the benefits far outweigh the little inconvenience of intentionally thinking positive thoughts.

We've learned about the negative thought patterns and some ways to counter them. To further ensure that you get effective results from these exercises, it is important to pinpoint the negative thought patterns that are deeply ingrained in your consciousness. Your thought patterns may continually revert to the negative if the old patterns are not first identified and dealt with.

The thought record

It's important to be aware of the negatives lurking in your consciousness. The thought record can help you uncover negative thoughts that you may have not been aware of and also help you change the negatives into positives. The steps involved in this exercise are:

1. Identify the negative thought that needs to be changed

2. Let go of the unwanted thought

3. Replace it with positive thoughts and proper
   coping measures

4. Incorporate the positive thoughts and coping
   measures in your life

Here's a simplified example:

The situation (What happened?)

I had an argument with my co-worker. He said my work was shabby and he embarrassed me in front of the other team members.

Initial thoughts (What thoughts popped in your mind when it happened?)

I actually thought he was right. My work is mediocre. I'm such a loser, I can't do anything right. When the boss finds out I'll lose my job.

Negative thought pattern (see chapter 2)

Self-labeling, filtering and catastrophizing

Source of negative belief (Why do you think this way? What experience in the past caused you to think this way?)

My dad used to call me a sure loser and he said I wouldn't be able to finish school or keep a job.

How can this kind of thinking affect you?

(What are the consequences of this negative thought pattern?)

I will fail to recognize my true potential. I will continue to let the past have its hold on me and I won't be able to move on. I will continue to believe a lie.

Alternative thought (What can you say to yourself to replace the negative belief?)

I have talents and skills and I can do my work well. I am not a loser, I can be a winner.

Action to take (What action will you take to

reinforce your new belief?)

I will not let criticism put me down because I know I can do a
good job. I will list the steps to improve my work and then take
action on them.

Make a thought record everyday for a few weeks. You'll soon recognize your usual negative thought patterns and learn to replace them with positive ones. Go back to your earlier notes and be aware of any improvements.

Now you are ready to practice other positive thinking exercises in different areas in your life.

With family and friends

Connect with other positive thinkers

Find the people who think positively and spend time with them. Let their optimism rub off on you. Staying with positive people is one way to reinforce your own positivity. There are people who make you feel refreshed after you've had a chat with or spent time with them. Enjoy your time with them and try to set appointments with them when you can.

Share the good times as well as the bad

What are friends for? Be ready to be there for a family member or friend. When you're experiencing a crisis, open up to someone you can trust. It is healthy to be able to unload your burdens and not keep them pent up inside. However, try not to dwell on the negative for too long. Get whatever it is off of you chest and then move on to a brighter more positive topic of conversation.

Do a good deed

You don't need to keep tabs on your good deeds. Reaching out to someone and doing something to make them happy will warm your heart as well. It doesn't have to be a big thing, simply saying hi and smiling could make somebody else's day. Look for little ways in which you could brighten up the lives of others.

Show gratitude

Many resentments and conflicts stem from one party's ingratitude. Saying thank you can quickly dissipate tension and give the other person affirmation.

Take note of people's positive traits

Taking note of people's positive traits helps you to steer away from dwelling on the negatives. When you remember a person's positive points, you'll be more tolerant and forgiving of their weaknesses. Compliment others sincerely and spread the positivity.

Count your blessings

Be thankful for every little thing. Always take mental notes of the good things in your life. Be thankful for the sunny weather, your good health and that you have family and friends who support you. Awareness of your blessings helps makes is easier to bear any challenges that come your way. Take a few minutes each morning to write down what you are grateful for and why you are looking forward to the day ahead, and then a few minutes at the end of the day to write down what was good about the day.

Don't let the little things cause permanent damage to your relationships

Count the cost before you lose your top. Is your son's messy room reason enough to alienate him? Learn to choose your battles and let go when you can. Think of the long term consequences of your loss of temper or self-control.

Have fun together

Let fun and childlike playfulness characterize your relationships. Having fun together melts barriers and makes everyone equal. Make an effort to be playful with your spouse, your children and all the other people around you.

At work

Maintain good posture

This may sound strange but keeping your back straight and your head high can do wonders. You circulation and balance will improve. You'll also feel more confident and energetic. If you sit for long periods, avoid slouching. When you stand tall or sit up straight, you send signals to your body, and to others around you, that you feel confident and optimistic.

Create a positive workspace

Fill your workspace with things that make you feel motivated yet relaxed. Display photos of people or things that lift your spirits.

Avoid party poopers

To maintain a positive disposition at work, try to steer away from people who drain your energy. Deal with them politely but be careful not to imbibe their negativity.

Don't be too hard on yourself

Resist the urge for self-blame and be your own number one fan instead. Don't beat yourself up for that one mistake. Accept that you do make mistakes and that you're not perfect. Nobody is.

Be on the lookout for opportunity

Instead of dwelling on how you screwed up, believe in yourself and focus on improving your work. Keep your eyes open for opportunities to advance as well as to learn, earn and contribute more.

Empathize

Make an effort to see things from your boss's or your coworker's point of view. Seeing things from other people's point of view and putting yourself in their shoes will make you more understanding and tolerant of differences. It will also help you accept your mistakes.

When facing challenging times

This too shall pass

No matter how tough, no matter how scary, no matter how painful; keep in mind that it will not be that way forever. Change is sure to come. It may take time but it will come. In the meantime, hold on to this hope and take things a step at a time.

Choose to be resilient

Be determined to survive and to emerge victorious. This is your chance to see how strong you can actually be.

Focus on the solution

Setting up a plan or steps to overcome a challenge can help remove your focus from the negatives. Taking steps toward a solution will give you a sense of control over the situation.

Baby steps

Trying to make ambitious changes can overwhelm and discourage you. Take baby steps and start small. Taking small and manageable steps will minimize stress. Before you know it, you will have already reached your goal.

Setting a Daily Routine of Thinking Positively

Start your day right

Determine the best way to set your mind on the right track at the very beginning of the day. Some people start with meditation or reading inspirational texts. Some start with stretching or yoga. Some start with music that makes them feel happy. Choose the best start of the day for you.

Exercise

Find a form of exercise that you enjoy -it could be anything from Tae Kwon Do and flamenco dancing to simply taking a stroll. Exercise lifts your spirits by easing tension in your body and releasing happy hormones.

Write a journal

Make a record of your positive experiences. Writing them down will reinforce your positivity. The entries can be short and simple. It shouldn't feel like a chore.

Set aside time to recharge

Find time for an activity that you find refreshing. It might be reading a book or listening to relaxing music. This is not a luxury, but rather a necessity when it comes to keeping a positive state of mind.

Believe that good things will happen

No matter what happens, the good times will still come. You might want to smile to yourself and say "Good things will happen today," as you walk out of your front door. This way you will face the day motivated and filled with a positive anticipation and expectation of what lies ahead.

Don't be overwhelmed by all the exercises listed here. Choose one or two and try them out, then gradually add more to your daily routine. Soon, your life will change and people will respond to you differently. You will look in the mirror and see a twinkle in your eye.

The aches and pains in your body will subside and you'll gain a spring in your step. Don't be surprised if opportunities seem to surge toward you. This is the beginning of something good!

<u>Conclusion</u>

I hope this book has given you a more thorough insight into positive thinking. Although it's sometimes thought of as something mystical and not based in reality, the truth is actually very different. True positive thinking is about taking responsibility for our lives and choosing to face our challenges with a positive mindset and take positive action to overcome them and achieve our goals. Although it's not always easy to remain positive, regularly checking in helps us stay on track and keep pushing forwards.

Good luck with overcoming your challenges and moving towards your own goals, no matter what they may be!

A message from the author, Jane Aniston

Finally, if you enjoyed this book, **please** take the time to post a review on Amazon. It will only take a couple of minutes and I'd be extremely grateful for your support.

Thank you again for your support.

Jane Aniston

FREE BONUS NUMBER!

As a free bonus, I've included a preview of one of my other best-selling books, "Overcoming Anxiety - Practical Approaches You Can Use To Manage Fear & Anxiety In The Moment & Long Term"! **Scroll to the end of this book to read it.**

ALSO...

be sure to check out my other books. Scroll to the back of this book for a list of other books written by me, along with download links.

Enjoy!

Jane Aniston

FREE BONUS!: Preview Of

"Overcoming Anxiety - Practical Approaches You Can Use To Manage Fear & Anxiety In The Moment & Long Term"

If you enjoyed this book, I have a little bonus for you; a preview of one of my other books "Overcoming Anxiety - Practical Approaches You Can Use To Manage Fear & Anxiety In The Moment & Long Term", which goes into more detail on how you can manage anxiety safely and naturally! Enjoy!

Short excerpt from Chapter 4

Lifestyle Changes for a Long-Term Solution

Overcoming anxiety over the long haul takes more than just a few quick fixes to quell the nerves; it requires making lifestyles changes. The changes that have to be made include getting more physically active, working on achieving optimal sleep patterns, learning to handle and minimize stress better, quitting (or at least heavily cutting down on) alcohol and smoking, cutting down on caffeinated beverages, and switching to a healthier eating habit. Long-term changes cannot happen overnight; it will require commitment and patience, as you gradually take realistic steps towards improving your mental and physical health.

Get More Active

Easily the most important and helpful thing you can incorporate into your life is a regular exercise routine. Living a sedentary lifestyle filled with stress will definitely contribute to more senseless worrying. On the other hand, frequent exercise has been proven in numerous studies to reduce anxiety symptoms. Your overall well-being will benefit due to exercise causing your body to release feel-good hormones and chemicals that will improve mood and promote relaxation.

If you have never exercised regularly in the past, you can start building the habit of being more active with simple activities that get you moving. Consider taking a 30-minute stroll around the neighborhood every morning before going to work, parking your car some distance from your destination and walking the rest of the way, taking the stairs over riding the escalator, going for a nature hike on the weekends or taking a longer than usual walk with your dog. Although these may seem like relatively minor steps, if you do them regularly you'll find yourself feeling more energized and building a higher level of self discipline. This in turn should not only allow you to move on to more strenuous exercise, but is also very likely to give you a mental boost and make you feel good about yourself.

Take Up a Formal Exercise Program

To obtain the full benefit of physical activity, consider allocating time for a formal exercise program. This involves a regular set of exercises which you have to take time out of your daily life for, such as lifting weights at the gym, attending an aerobics class, or taking up a sport. It can be challenging to commit yourself to exercising, especially when you have work-life demands to fulfill. That being said, where there is a will, there is definitely a way! Think of the money spent on health club memberships and time allocated to exercising as an investment in yourself, because your well-being matters. Again, the benefits of regular excursus have been proven by numerous studies to lead to HUGE benefits; some studies have even found that exercising regularly can be as effective as taking pharmaceutical drugs when combatting conditions such as anxiety and depression!

Try Yoga

A non-religious spiritual practice that originates from India thousands of years ago, yoga has often been touted as the comprehensive mind, body and spirit workout. These claims are far from an exaggeration though. Academic research in the western world since the 1970s has considered yoga one of the best possible treatments for depression and anxiety. Since the early 2000s, yoga has gained worldwide popularity as a fitness lifestyle practice, which has lead to it becoming a staple program offered in many gyms and health clubs. There are event studios and vacation retreats dedicated to the practice, offering courses to yogis of all levels.

In a nutshell, yoga is a system of exercise that comprises deep meditation, breathing techniques and series of physical workouts in the form of postures known as *Asana*. Some of the more orthodox yoga schools and teachers would even encourage students to incorporate the spiritual (but non-religious) elements of yoga. With consistent practice, one can reap the multiple benefits of yoga, which include:

* A calm, steady and equanimous mind

* Improved mood

- Hormonal balance

- Greater flexibility and range of motion

- Greater spinal and joint health

- Improved strength and muscle tone

- Steady weight loss and maintenance

- Lowered risk of sports injury

- Lowered risk of various chronic illnesses

- Improved self-confidence

- An overall brighter outlook on life

Those who are unfamiliar with yoga may be intimidated by the demonstration of postures that seem to require a vast amount of strength and flexibility. That should not deter you from trying out this transformative workout, because there are literally hundreds of yoga postures and they vary in difficulty. Moreover, a competent instructor – known as a guru – can guide a beginner through the practice, providing modifications to difficult postures, so the student can ease themselves into the practice.

The practice of yoga has a long history, which has branched into different traditions and styles. Certain styles are more suited to relaxation, whereas some are more physically demanding. If you intend to begin practicing yoga, take time to choose a studio and teacher that offers the style of yoga best suited to your needs.

(Chapter 4 continues in the full book)

Short excerpt from Chapter 5

Cognitive Behavioral Therapy and Anxiety Disorders

Because anxiety disorders vary significantly in severity among sufferers, the treatment administered normally depends on each individual's case. One of the most common and renowned treatments for anxiety disorders is Cognitive Behavioral Therapy (CBT). It has been scientifically tested and found to be effective in hundreds of clinical trials for remedying many different mental disorders. Unlike other forms of psychotherapy, CBT is more problem-solving oriented. Patients learn specific skills that involve identifying distorted thinking patterns, modifying beliefs, relating to others differently and changing behaviors – skills which can be used for the rest of their lives.

This chapter will give you the basics on CBT, so that you will know what to expect from this treatment when seeking professional medical help for anxiety disorder.

The Theory Behind CBT

Simply put, CBT is based on the cognitive model of how the way we perceive things and situations can influence the way we feel and behave. In other words, if you interpret a situation negatively, you might feel negative emotions as a result and that in turn will lead you to behave in a certain manner. For example, someone who is obligated to attend a party might think, "This is an excellent opportunity to meet people and network!". This outlook will leave them looking forward to the event. Another person, who is less keen may think "I don't know most of the guests, so I just want to get it over and done with as quickly as possible". As you can see, it is not a situation itself that directly affects how people feel emotionally, but rather, our thoughts and perception about that situation.

When people are in distress, their perspectives and judgments are often clouded and inaccurate, causing their thoughts and imagination to run wild. CBT helps people identify thoughts that are causing them anxiety and evaluate how realistic the thoughts actually are when examined more closely. Patients then learn to change their distorted thinking patterns and adopt a more realistic approach.

(Chapter 5 continues in the full book)

Check out the rest of "Overcoming Anxiety - Practical Approaches You Can Use To Manage Fear & Anxiety In The Moment & Long Term" on the Amazon store by clicking here!

Check Out My Other Books!

Understanding Anxiety

Overcoming Anxiety

Depression - Practical & Natural Approaches You Can Use To Cure Depression In The Moment & Long Term

Cognitive Behavioral Therapy - A Practical Guide To C.B.T. For Overcoming Anxiety, Depression, Addictions & Other Psychological Conditions

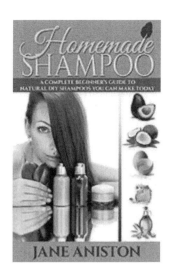

Homemade Shampoo (Includes 34 Organic Shampoo Recipes!)

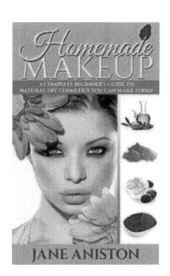

Homemade Makeup (Includes 28 Organic Makeup Recipes!)

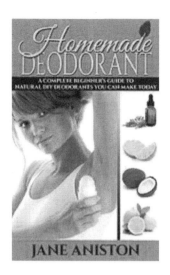

Homemade Deodorant (Includes 20 Organic Deodorant Recipes!)

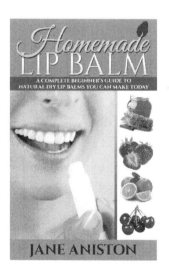

Homemade Lip Balm (Includes 22 Organic Lip Balm Recipes!)

Homemade Bath Salts (Includes 35 Organic Bath Salt Recipes!)

All books available as digital downloads and printed books

Printed in Great Britain
by Amazon